Donated with funds from
Neva Lomason Memorial Library
Penny Box
through the Friends of the Library
Matching Gift Program, 2009

W9-AET-850

WEST GA REG LIB SYS
Neva Lomason
Memorial Library

A+ books ™

Alphabet Books

Farms ABC

An Alphabet Book

by B. A. Hoena

Consulting Editor:
Gail Saunders-Smith, PhD

Capstone press

Mankato, Minnesota

A is for awake.

It's early in the morning,
but farmers are awake.
They have lots of work to do
throughout the day.

B is for barn.

A barn is a home for the animals on a farm. Inside, you might see cows, pigs, or sheep.

C is for corn.

Farmers grow corn for food.
The field corn shown here
will be a farm animal's meal.

D is for dog.

Some farm dogs have jobs. Border collies round up sheep and show them where to go. **ARF! ARF!**

E is for eggs.

Chickens lay eggs in straw nests. Farmers collect and sell the eggs, so you can eat them for breakfast.

F is for fence.

Farmers put up fences around fields.
Fences keep animals from roaming
too far from home.

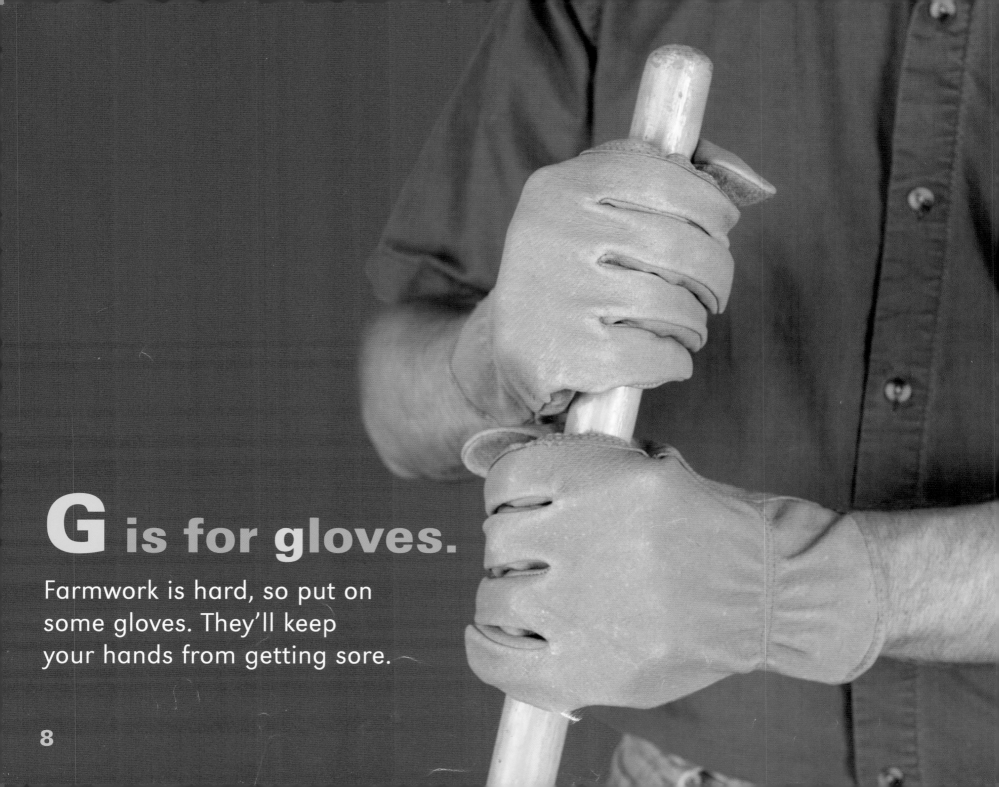

G is for gloves.

Farmwork is hard, so put on some gloves. They'll keep your hands from getting sore.

H is for hay.

Hay is dried grass. Someday soon, these round bales of hay will be food for farm animals.

I is for irrigation.

No, it's not raining. A farmer is irrigating a field. Farmers use irrigation to water their crops.

J is for jars.

People can foods, such as cucumbers, beans, and corn. Food stored in jars can be eaten any time of year.

K is for kittens.

Kittens roam about farms.
They like to hide and play
and chase after mice. **MEOW!**

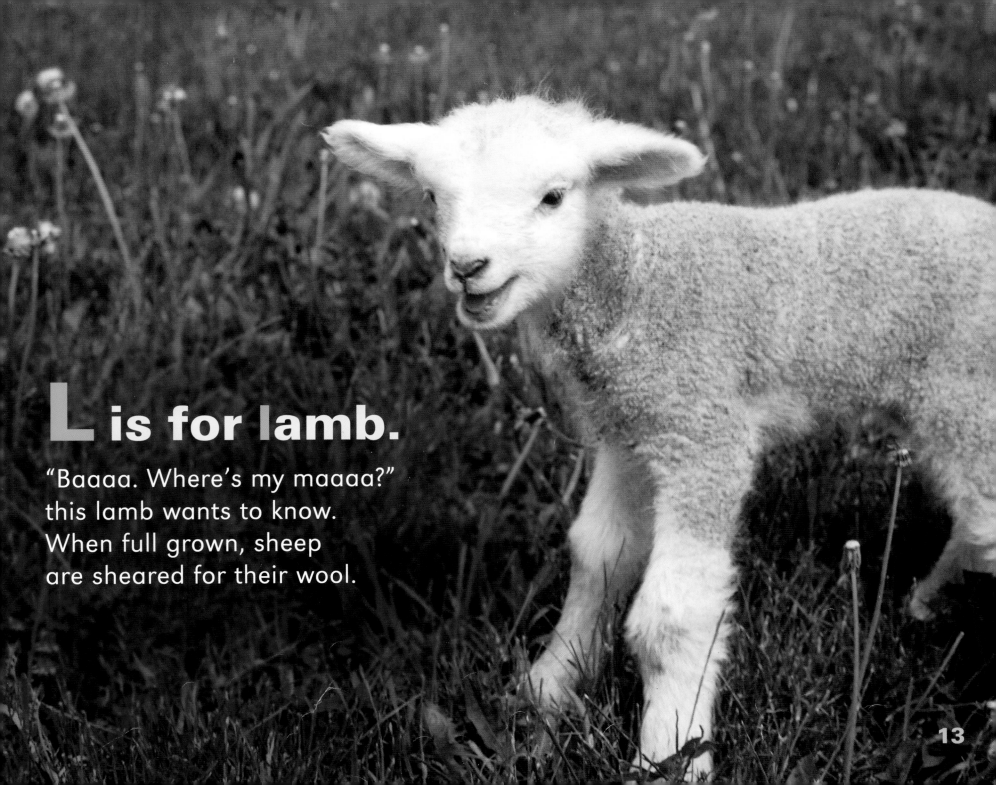

L is for lamb.

"Baaaa. Where's my maaaa?"
this lamb wants to know.
When full grown, sheep
are sheared for their wool.

M is for milk.

On dairy farms, farmers raise cows for their milk. Milk is used to make butter and cheese. Milk can also be a tasty drink.

N is for neigh.

"Neigh," is what horses say.
Horses once were raised to work
on farms. Now most horses
are raised for people to ride.

O is for oats.

Most oats that farmers grow are meals for animals. But people also eat this grain as oatmeal.

P is for pig.

Pigs sniff and snort as they roam about. Farmers raise them for meat called pork. **OINK! OINK!**

Q is for quack.

"Quack! Quack!" What's that?
Ducks are farm animals too.
Farmers raise ducks for feathers,
eggs, and meat.

R is for rooster.

Listen to the rooster crow.
He wants everyone to know
when the sun rises.
COCK-A-DOODLE-DOO!

S is for silo.

Look up high! That silo touches the sky. Silos are tall, round buildings used to store food for farm animals.

T is for tractor.

Tractors are important farm tools.
They pull wagons and machines
that farmers need to do their work.

U is for underground.

Farmers plant seeds underground.
As seeds grow, roots dig deep
into the soil, and leafy shoots
reach toward the sky.

V is for vegetables.

Farmers grow vegetables,
such as carrots, lettuce,
and beans. What vegetables
do you like to eat?

W is for wagons.

Farmers use wagons for hauling.
Wagons carry corn, hay, and other
heavy loads around the farm.

X is for fix.

Oh no, the machine won't go!
When something breaks
on the farm, farmers need
to know how to fix it.

25

Y is for year.

Farmers do different jobs
throughout the year.
They plant seeds in spring.
In fall, they harvest crops.

Z is for graze.

It's been a long day on the farm.
Now it's suppertime. Hungry cows
roam into the field to graze.
MOOOOOO!

Fun Facts about Farms

A dairy cow produces about 100 glasses of milk a day.

The kernels on ears of corn always grow in an even number of rows.

Tomatoes are actually fruits. Cucumbers and peppers are also fruits. Fruits are the edible parts of plants in which seeds grow.

Did you think that only cows eat grass? Wheat is a type of grass that people eat. It is used to make bread.

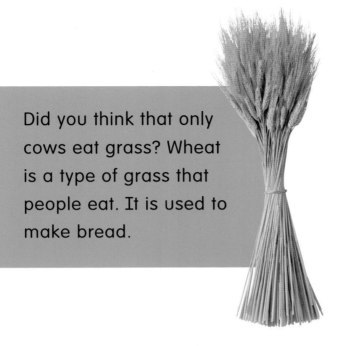

California produces more agricultural products than any other state.

There are more than 10 million horses in the United States. But China, Brazil, and Mexico all have more horse farms than the United States.

Most hens lay five eggs a week. That equals 260 eggs a year.

Glossary

can (KAN)—to preserve food in a jar

dairy (DAIR-ee)—having to do with milk products; dairy farmers raise cows for their milk.

grain (GRAYN)—the seed of a cereal plant, such as oats and wheat

graze (GRAYZ)—to eat plants that are growing in a field

harvest (HAR-vist)—to collect and gather crops

irrigation (ihr-uh-GAY-shuhn)—the process of supplying water to crops

shear (SHIHR)—to cut off or trim; a farmer shears a sheep's wool so it can be used to make cloth.

shoot (SHOOT)—a plant part that is just beginning to grow

Read More

Braidich, Shelby. *Meet Me on the Farm: Learning the Long E Sound.* PowerPhonics. New York: PowerKids Press, 2002.

Leeper, Angela. *Farm.* Field Trip! Chicago: Heinemann, 2004.

Scott, Janine. *Farm Friends.* Spyglass Books. Minneapolis: Compass Point Books, 2002.

Internet Sites

FactHound offers a safe, fun way to find Internet sites related to this book. All of the sites on FactHound have been researched by our staff.

Here's how:
1. Visit *www.facthound.com*
2. Type in this special code **0736836640** for age-appropriate sites. Or enter a search word related to this book for a more general search.
3. Click on the **Fetch It** button.

FactHound will fetch the best sites for you!

Index

A+ Books are published by Capstone Press,
151 Good Counsel Drive, P.O. Box 669, Mankato, Minnesota 56002.
www.capstonepress.com

Copyright © 2005 Capstone Press. All rights reserved.
No part of this publication may be reproduced in whole or in part, or stored in a retrieval system, or transmitted in any form or by any means, electronic, mechanical, photocopying, recording, or otherwise, without written permission of the publisher. For information regarding permission, write to Capstone Press, 151 Good Counsel Drive, P.O. Box 669, Dept. R, Mankato, Minnesota 56002.
Printed in the United States of America

1 2 3 4 5 6 10 09 08 07 06 05

Library of Congress Cataloging-in-Publication Data
Hoena, B. A.
    Farms ABC: An Alphabet Book / by B. A. Hoena; consulting editor, Gail Saunders-Smith.
    p. cm.—(A+ Books. Alphabet Books)
    Includes bibliographical references and index.
    ISBN-13: 978-0-7368-3664-7 (hardcover)
    ISBN-10: 0-7368-3664-0 (hardcover)
    1. Agriculture—Juvenile literature. 2. Farms—Juvenile literature. 3. English language—Alphabet—Juvenile literature. I. Saunders-Smith, Gail. II. Title. III. Series.
S519.H575 2005
428.1'3—dc22
                                       2004015233

Summary: Introduces farms through high-quality photographs and brief text that uses one word relating to farms for each letter of the alphabet.

Credits
Amanda Doering, editor; Heather Kindseth, set designer; Jennifer Bergstrom, book designer; Kelly Garvin, photo researcher; Scott Thoms, photo editor

Photo Credits
Artville, LLC, 28 (corn); BananaStock Ltd., 29 (horse); Brand X Pictures/Alley Cat Productions, 18; Bruce Coleman Inc./Hans Reinhard, 19; Bruce Coleman Inc./Janis Burger, 10; Bruce Coleman Inc./J.C. Carton, 15; Capstone Press/Karon Dubke, 8, 11, 20, 21, 23, 25; Color-Pic Inc./E.R. Degginger, 13; Corbis/Darrell Gulin, 3; Corbis/Japack Company, 14; Corbis/Ron Watts, 9; Corel, 28 (dairy cow); David R. Frazier Photolibrary, 24; Digital Vision, 1, 5, 17; Image Source/elektraVision, cover; Index Stock Imagery/Diaphor Agency, 6; Index Stock Imagery/Lynn Stone, 27; Index Stock Imagery/Wilson Goodrich, 12; John Blasdel, 22; OneBlueShoe, 7; Photodisc, 28 (tomatoes), 29 (wheat, eggs); Richard Hamilton Smith, 2, 4, 16; SuperStock/Americana Images, 26

Note to Parents, Teachers, and Librarians

Farms ABC: An Alphabet Book uses colorful photographs and a nonfiction format to introduce children to characteristics about farms while building a mastery of the alphabet. This book is designed to be read independently by an early reader or to be read aloud to a pre-reader. The images help early readers and listeners understand the text and concepts discussed. The book encourages further learning by including the following sections: Fun Facts about Farms, Glossary, Read More, Internet Sites, and Index. Early readers may need assistance using these features.

6/1/2022: Scribble in ink — inside back cover.
WGRL-NL SC

WGRL-HQ EASY
31057010768318
E HOENA
Hoena, B. A.
Farms ABC : an alphabet book

Hoena, B. A.
WEST GA REGIONAL LIBRARY SYS